COLOURFUL WORDS FROM AROUND THE WORLD

A SWEAR WORD COLOURING BOOK FOR ADULTS

COLOURFUL WORDS FROM
AROUND THE WORLD

A SWEAR WORD COLOURING
BOOK FOR ADULTS

ILLUSTRATIONS

AFRIKAANS – Jou Ma Naai Vir Viskoppe Daar By Die Docks
AMERICAN – Hoe Bag
AUSTRALIAN – Derro
DANISH – Din Kaelling
FRENCH – Ferme Ta Gueule
GAELIC – Gabh Suas Ort Fein
GERMAN – Schlampe
GREEK – Malaka
HAWAIIAN – Ahu Ka 'Ala'Ala
HINDI - Padma
ICELANDIC – Krakkmella
JAMAICAN (PATOIS) – Suck Yuh Madda
JAPANESE – Baka Ka
MEXICAN – No Me Chingues
NORWEGIAN – Fittetryne
POLISH – Pizda
PORTUGUESE – Puta Merde
RUSSIAN – Dolbo Yeb
SPANISH – Pajero
TURKISH – Siktir Git

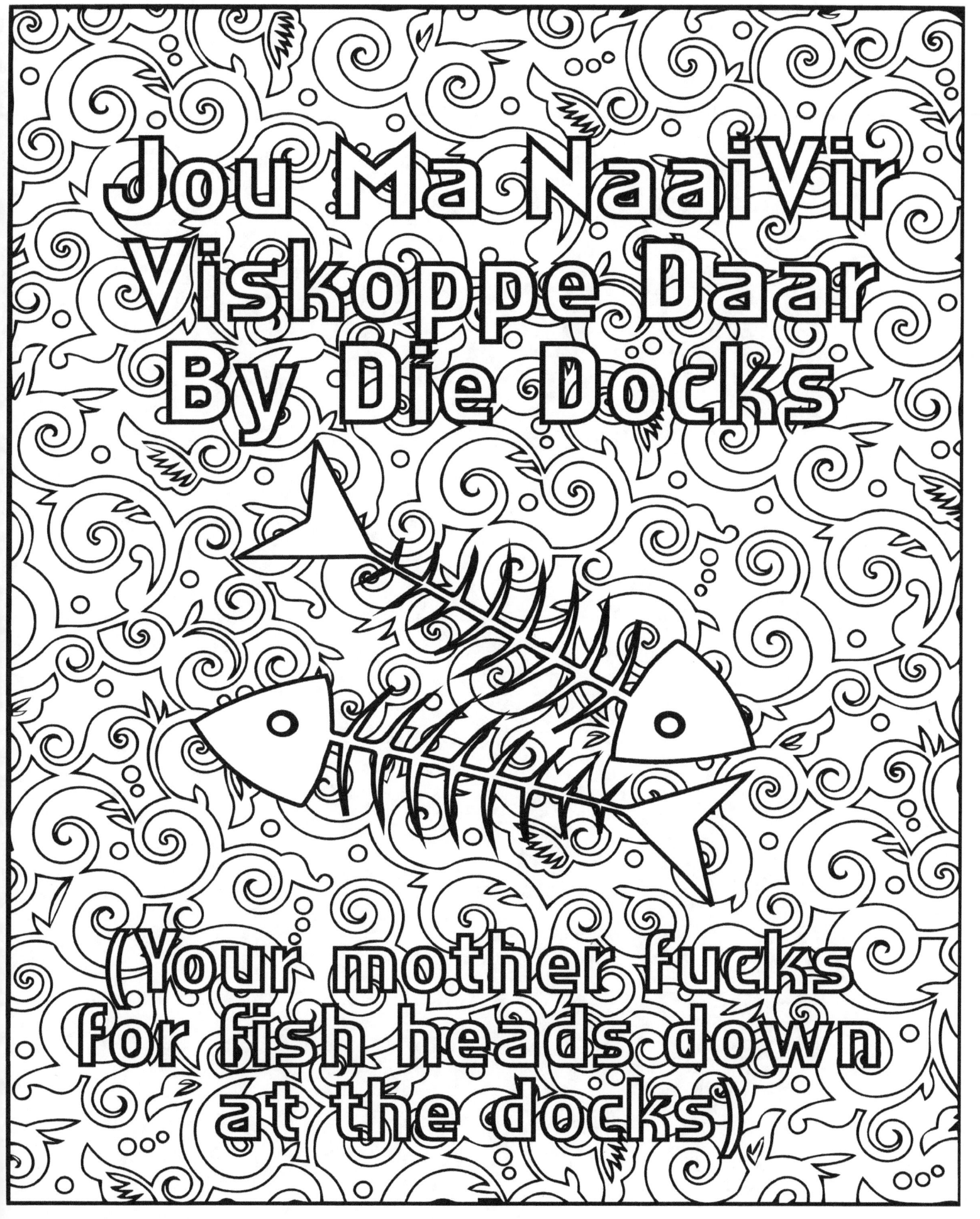

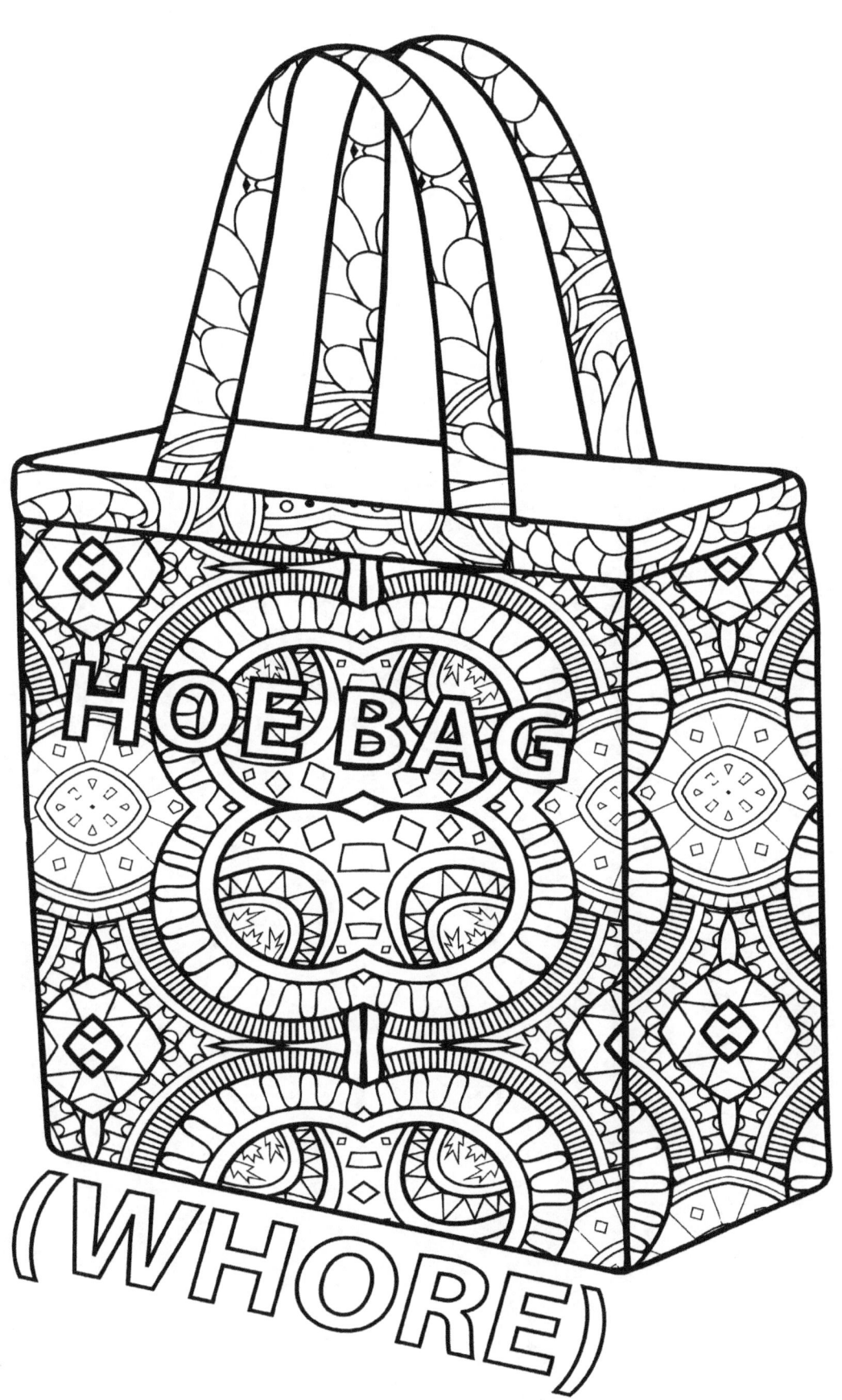

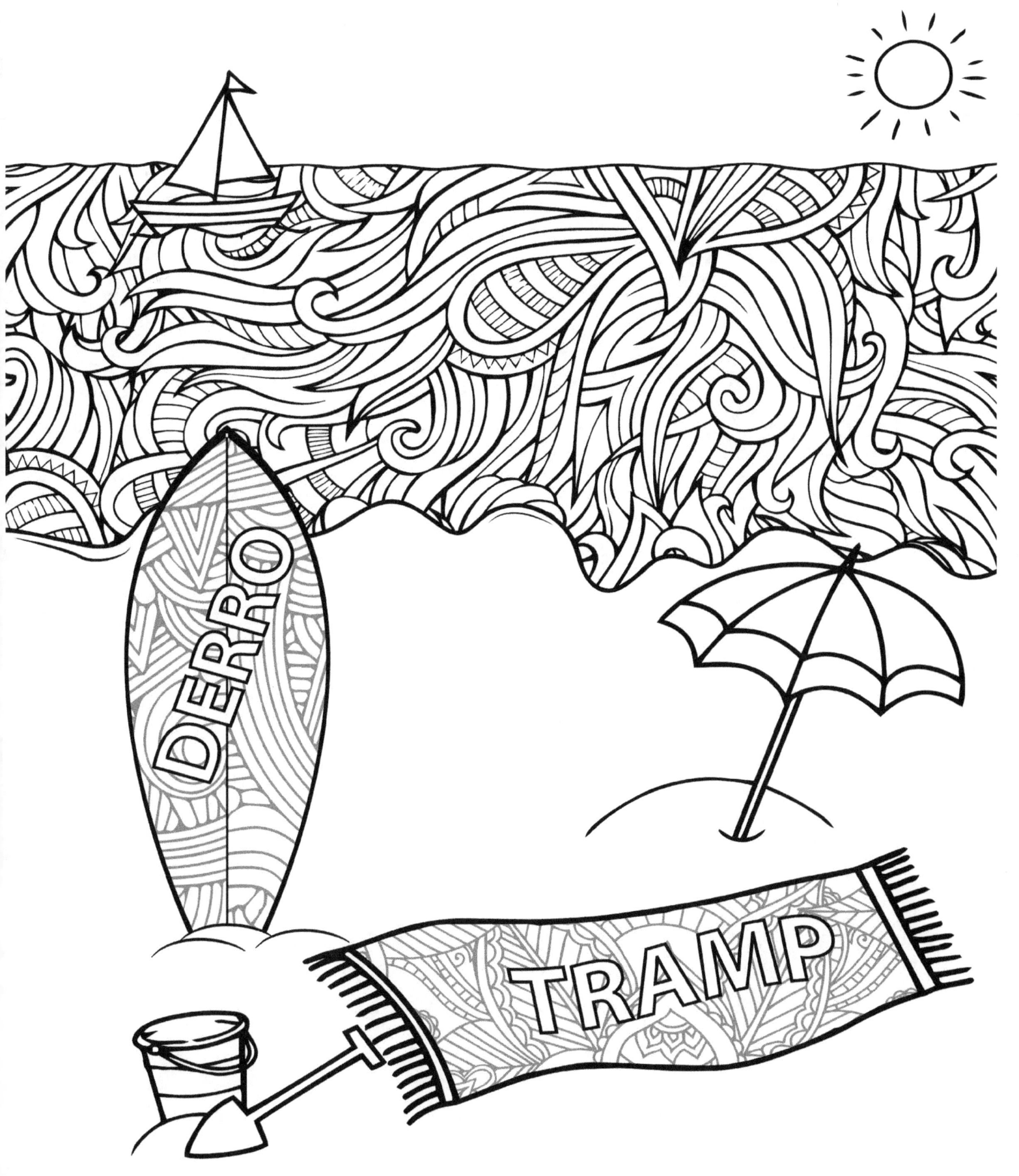

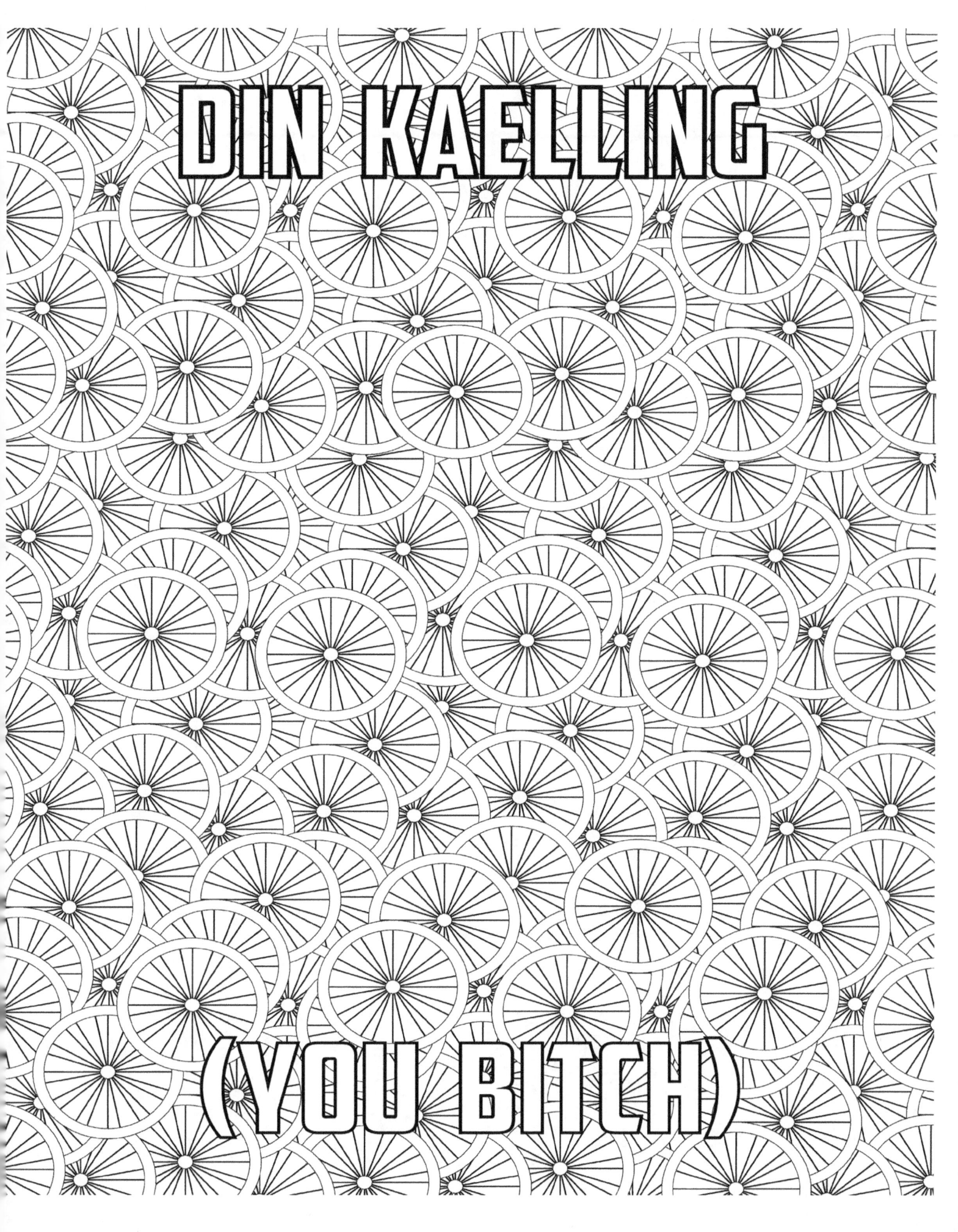

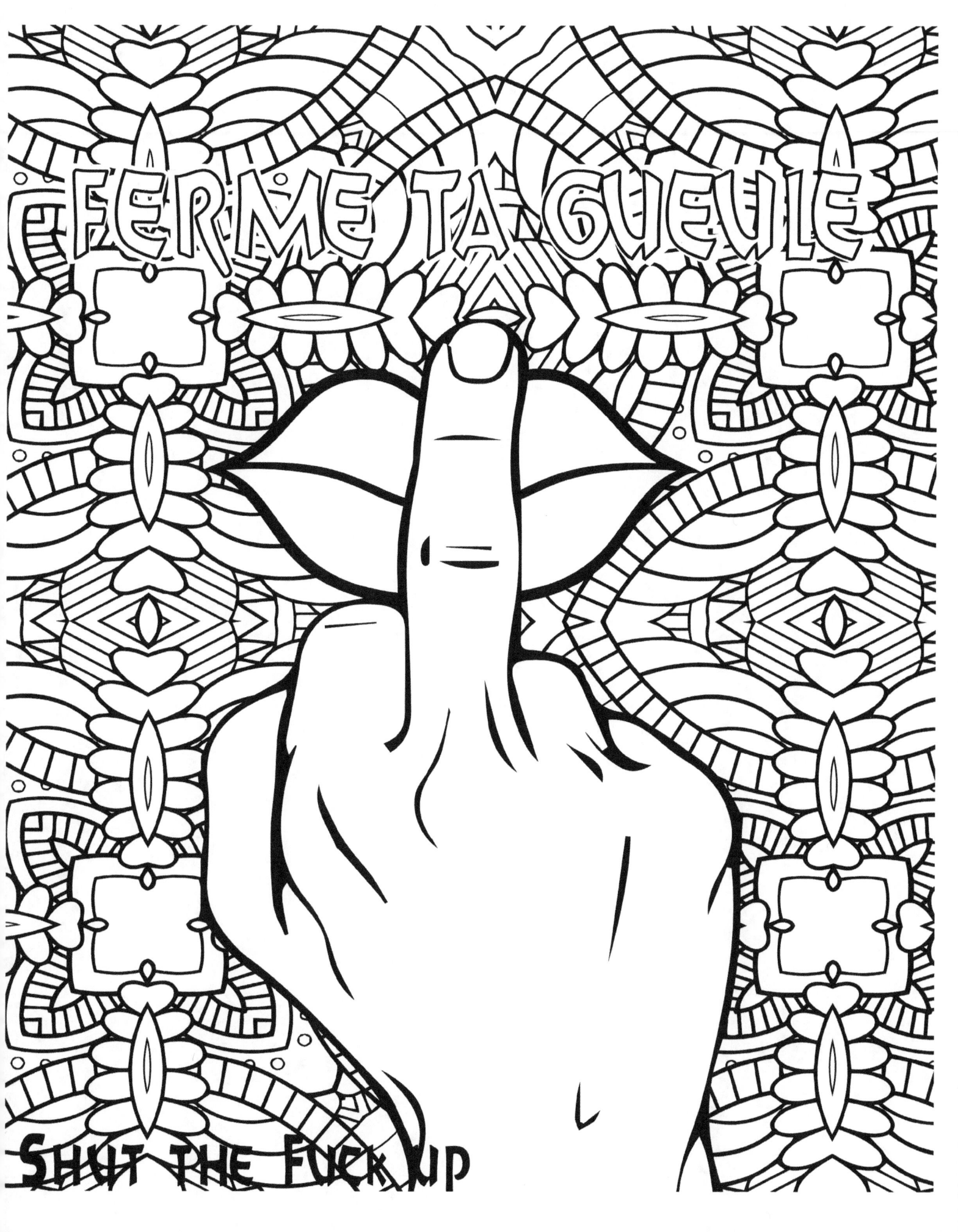

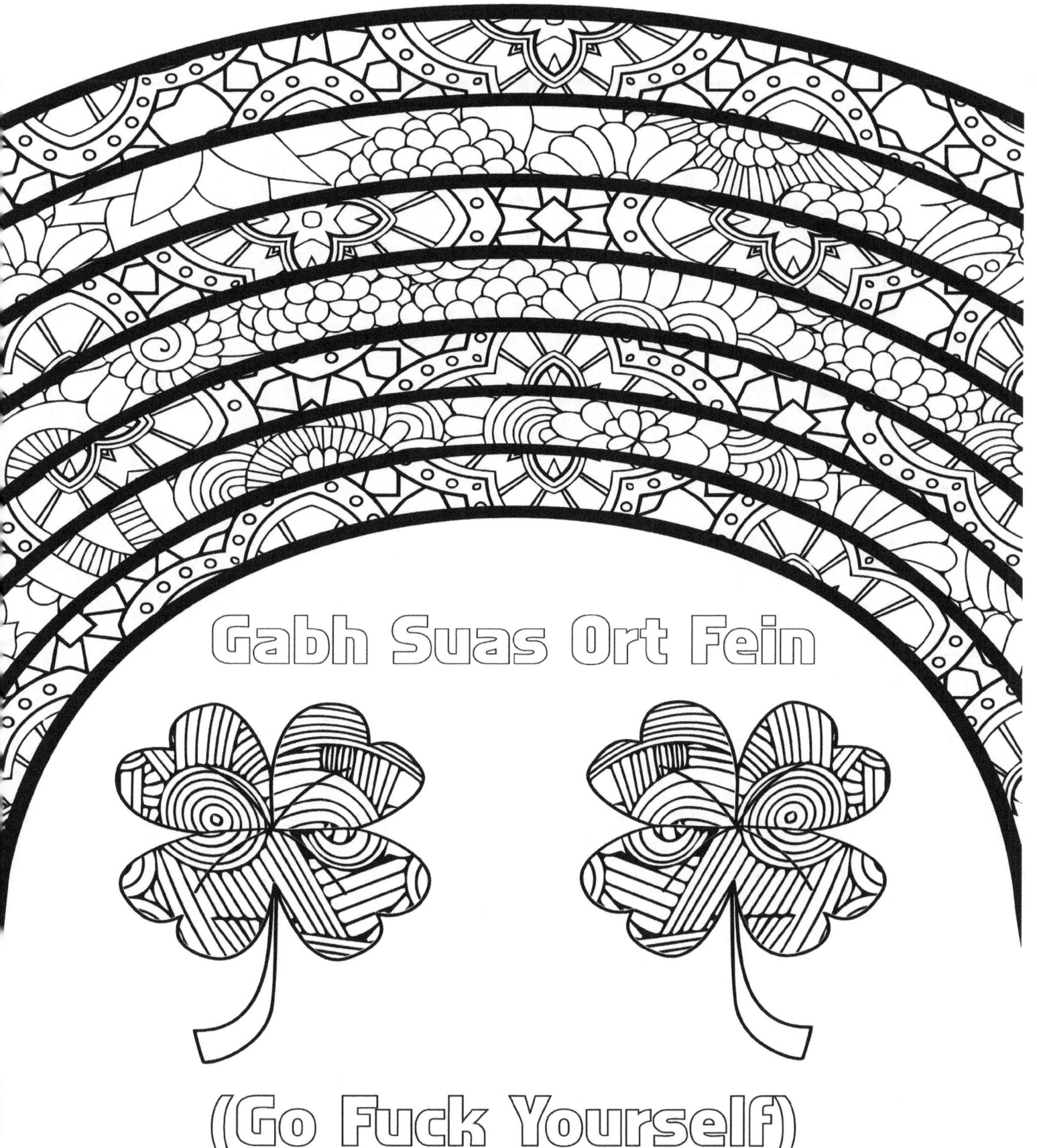

Gabh Suas Ort Fein

(Go Fuck Yourself)

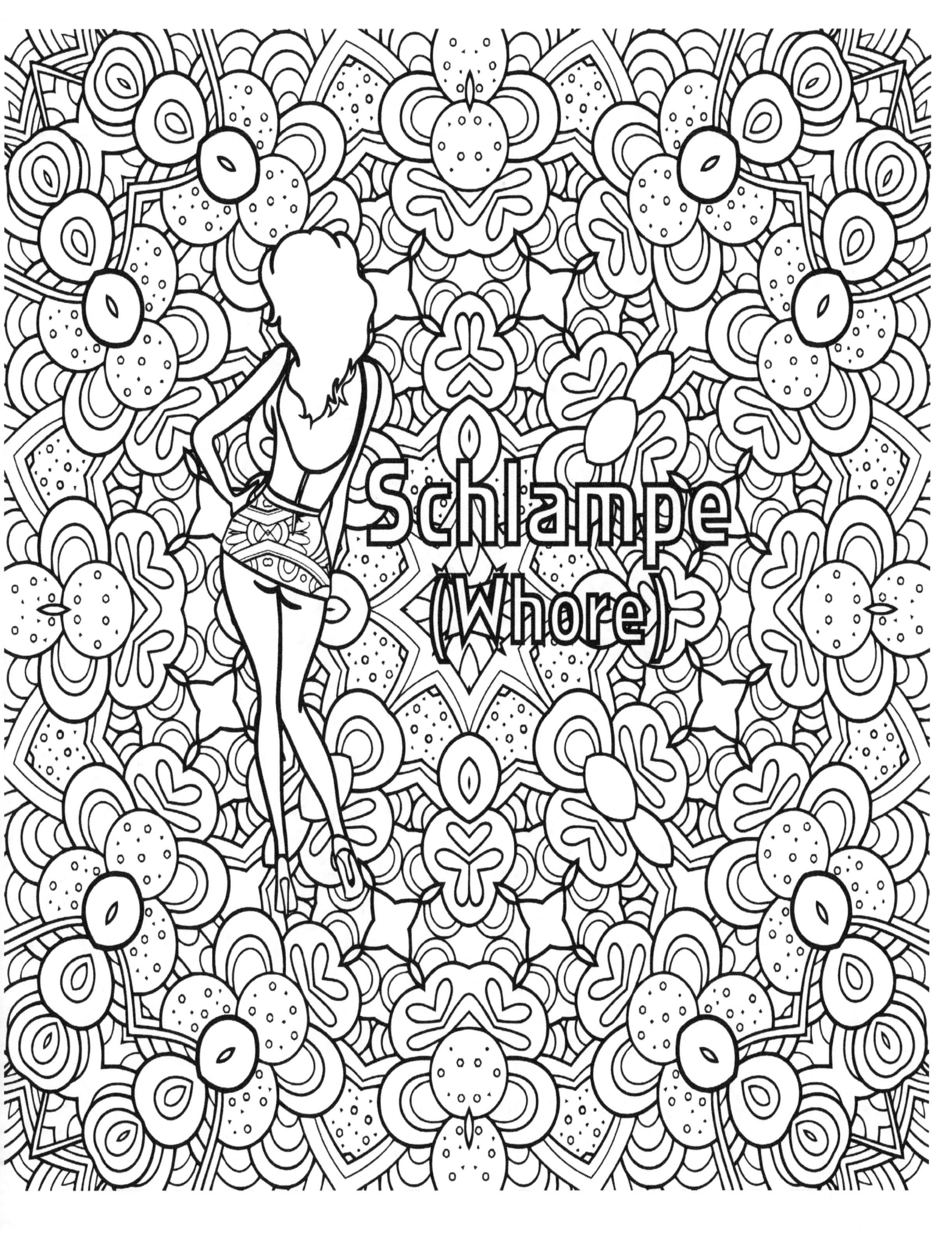

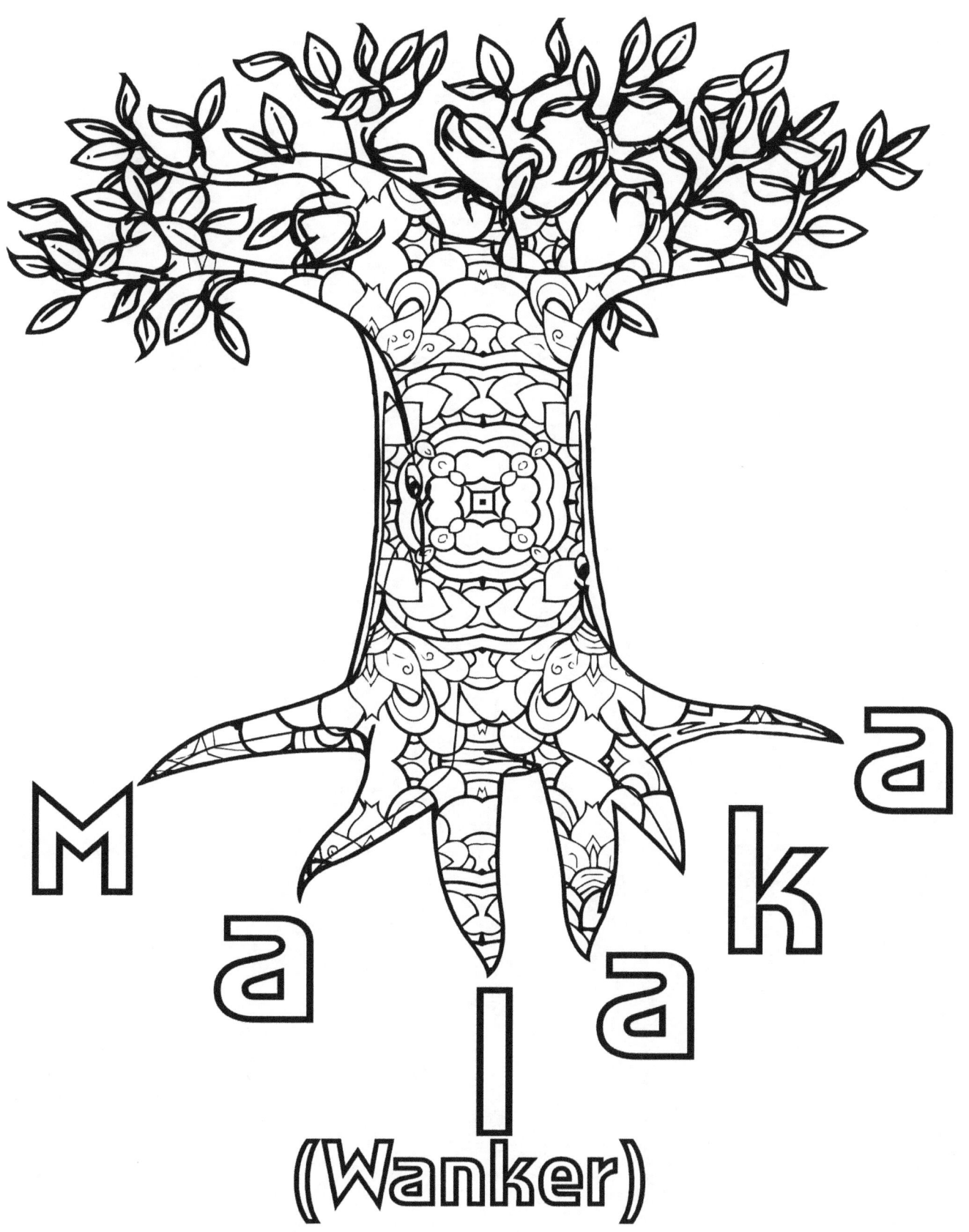

Malaka

(Wanker)

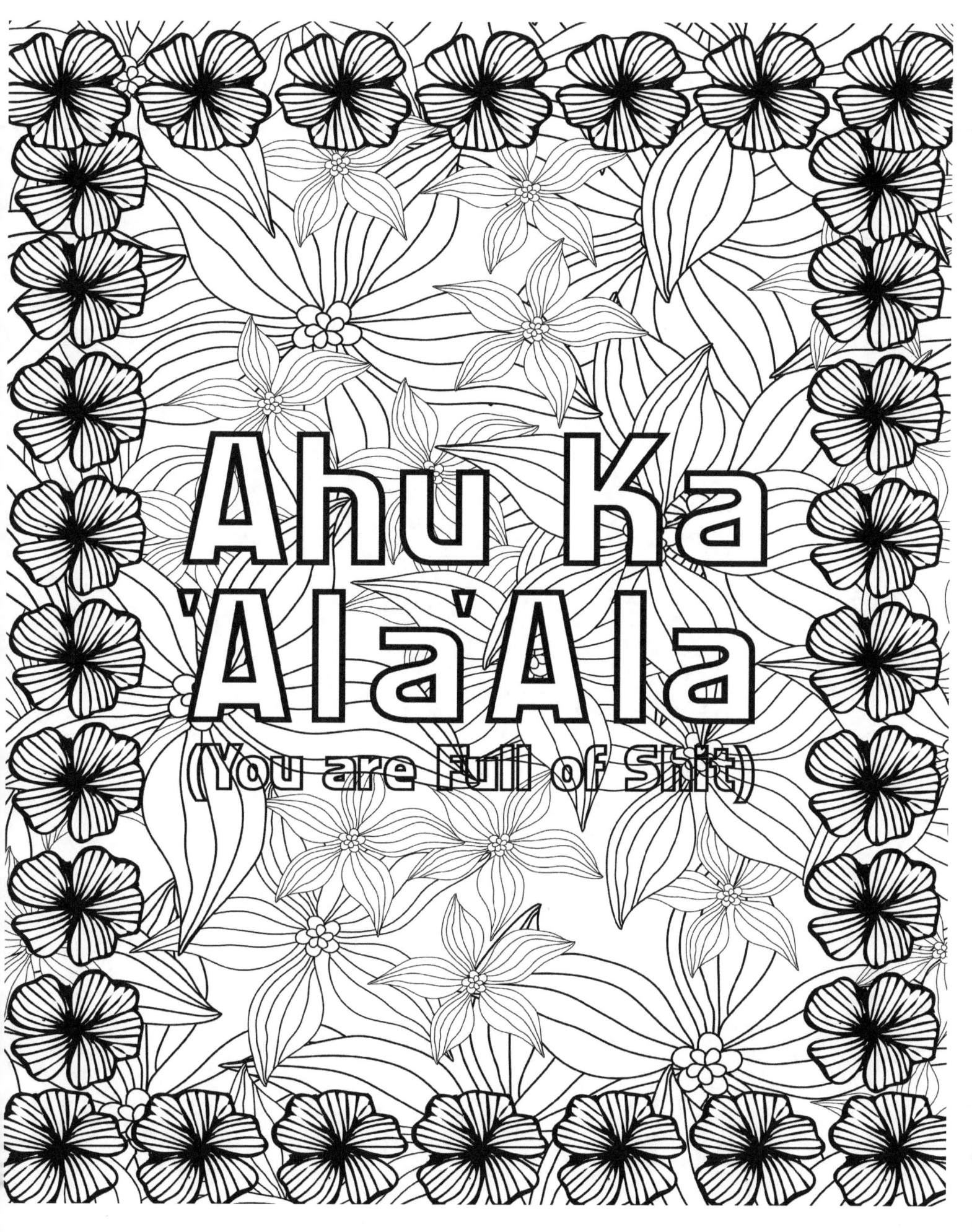

Krakkmella
(Crack Whore)

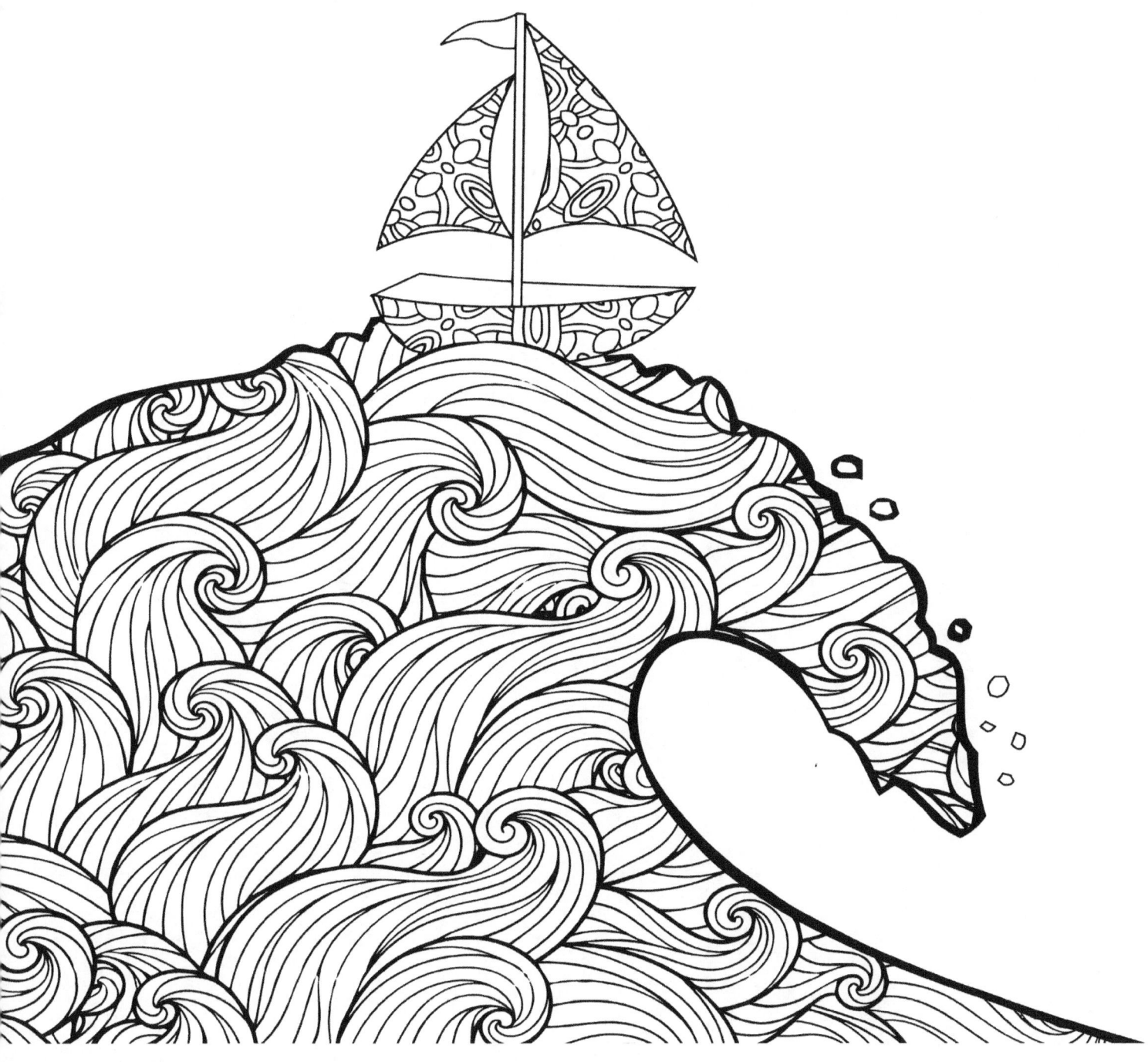

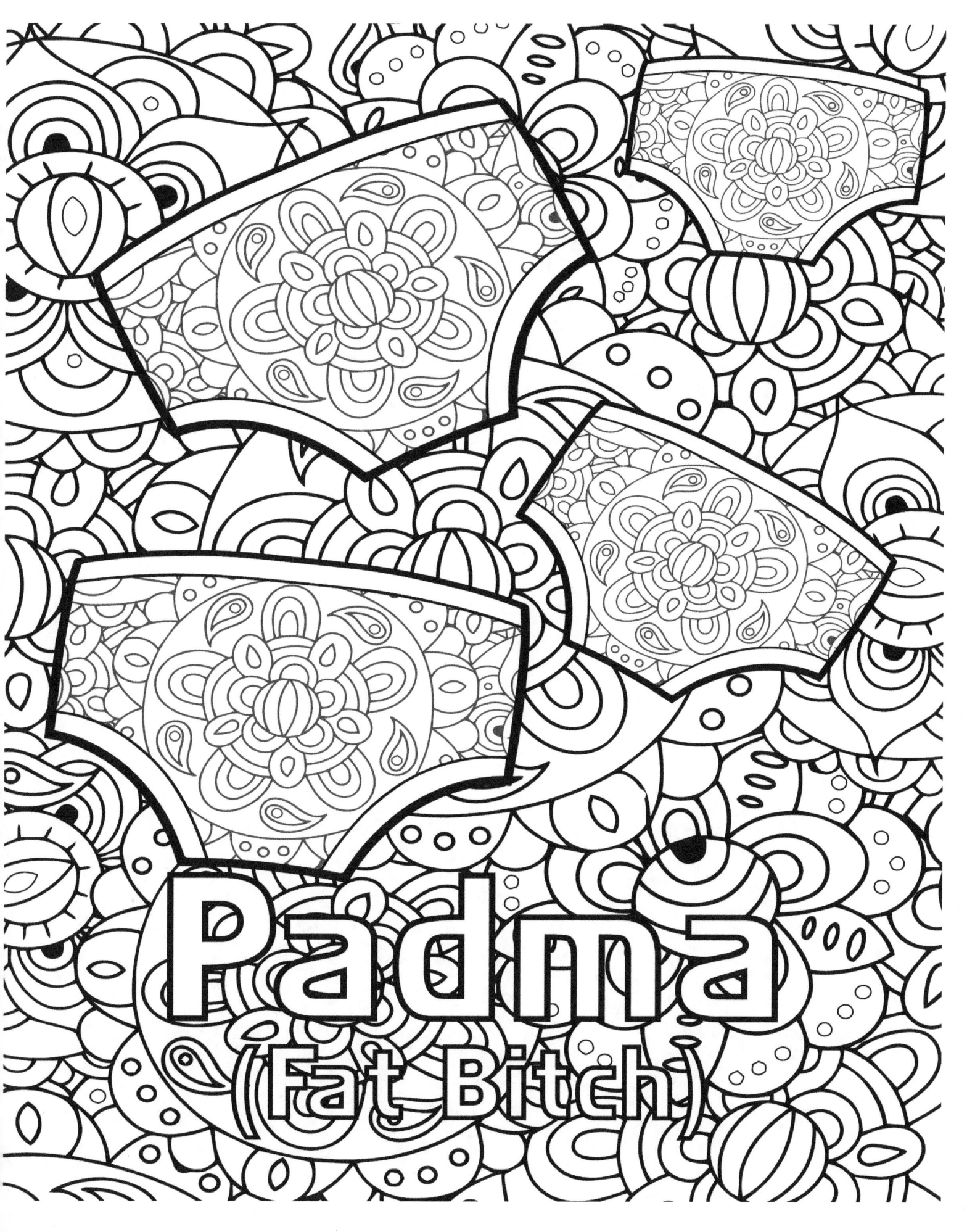

Padma

(Fat Bitch)

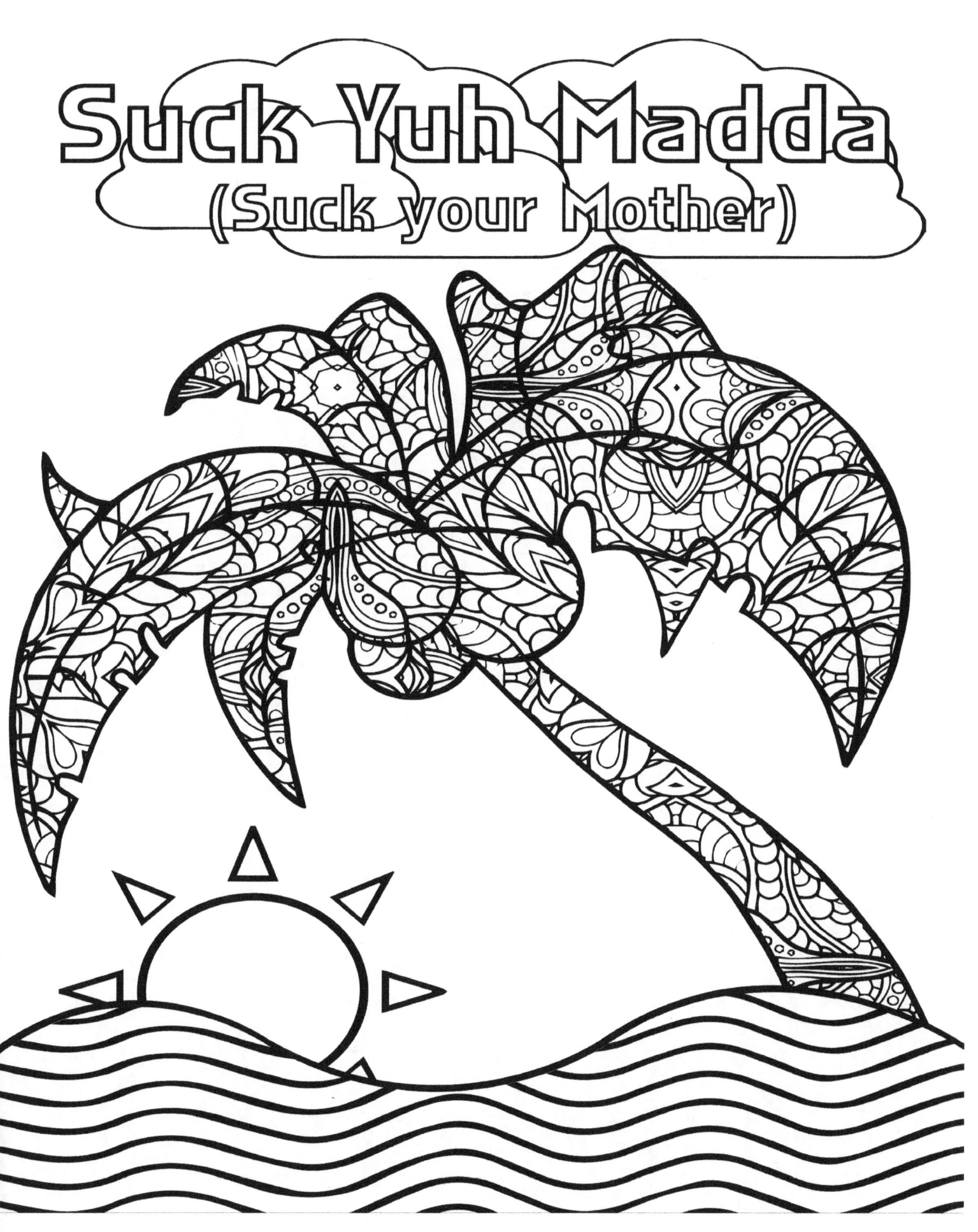

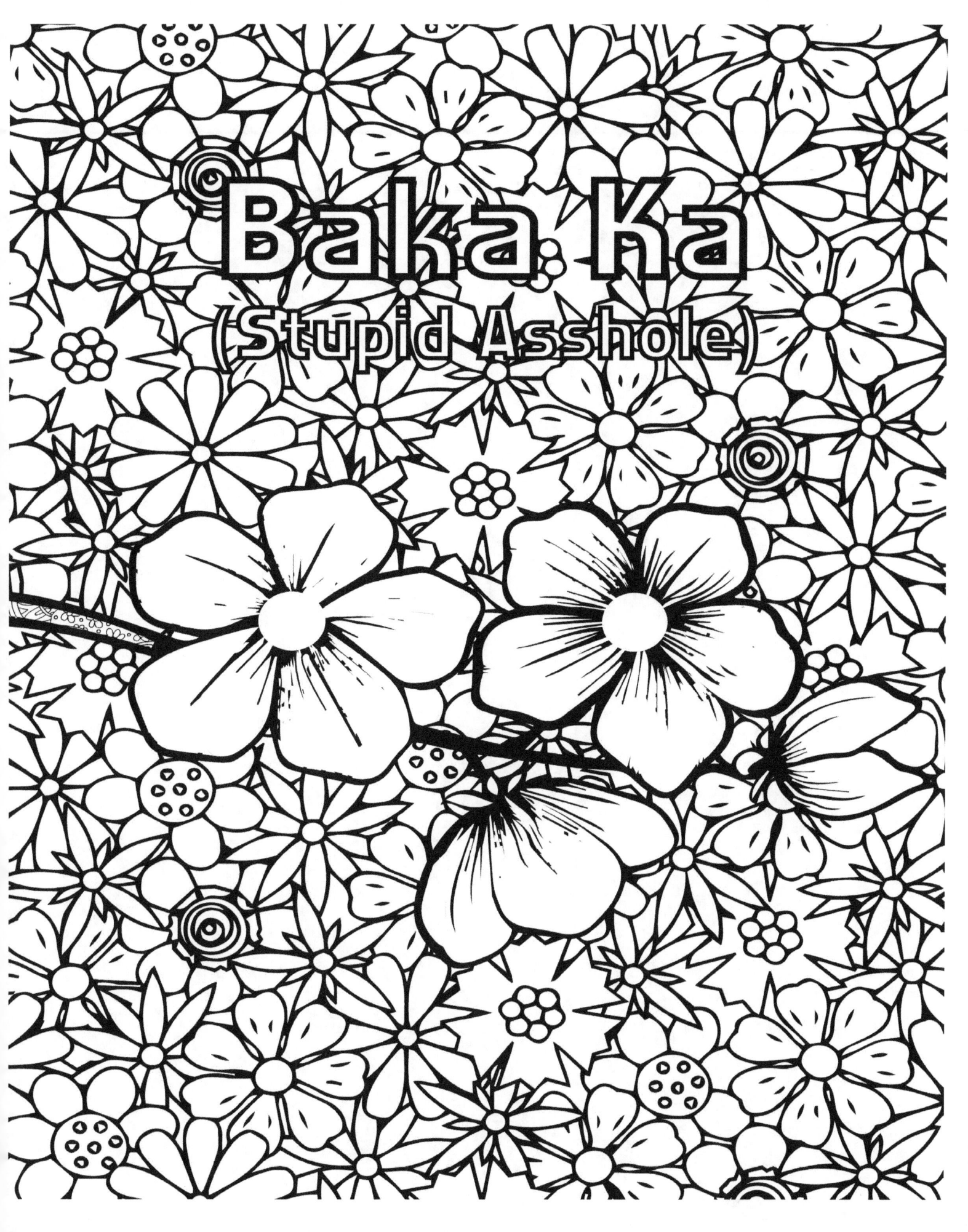

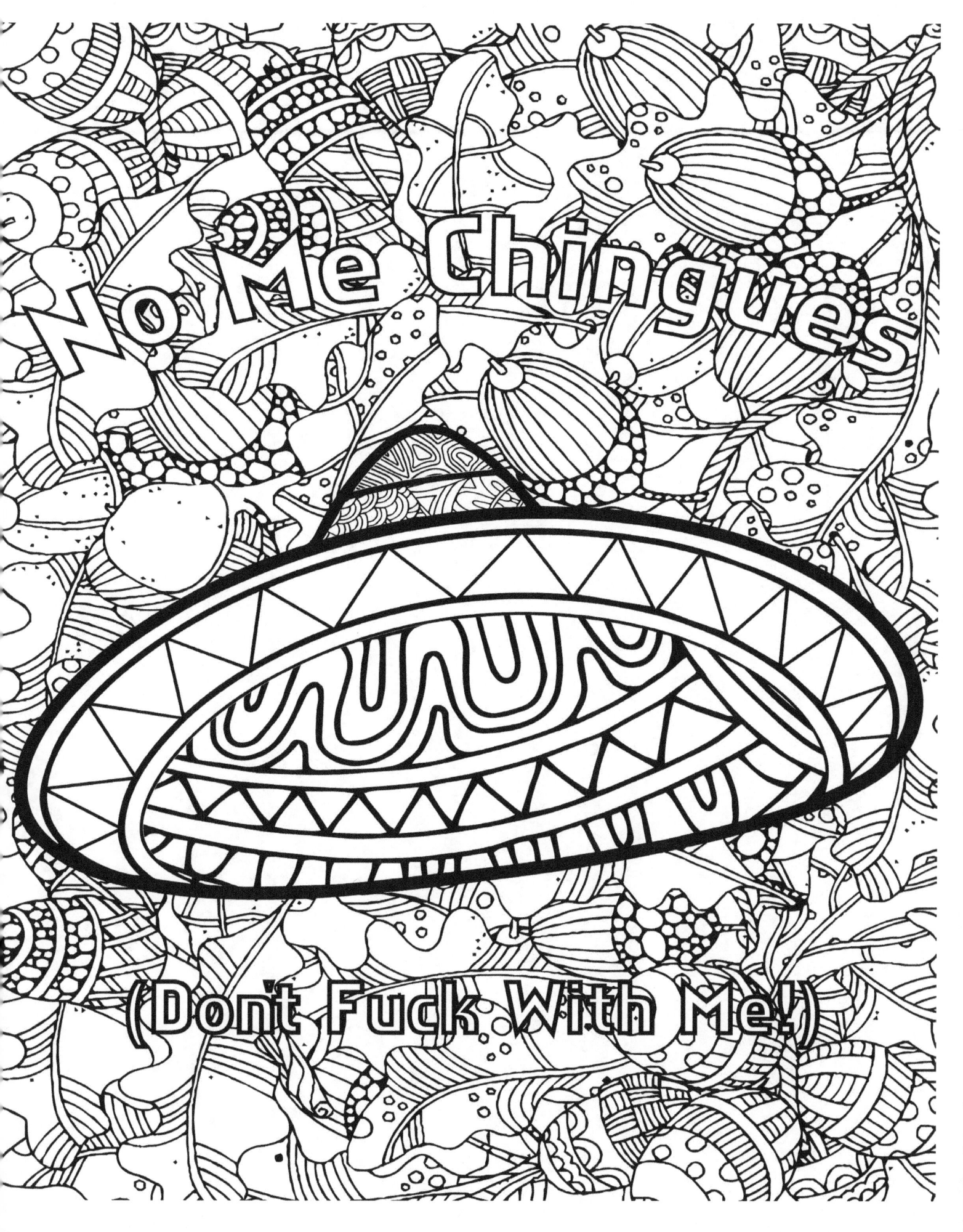

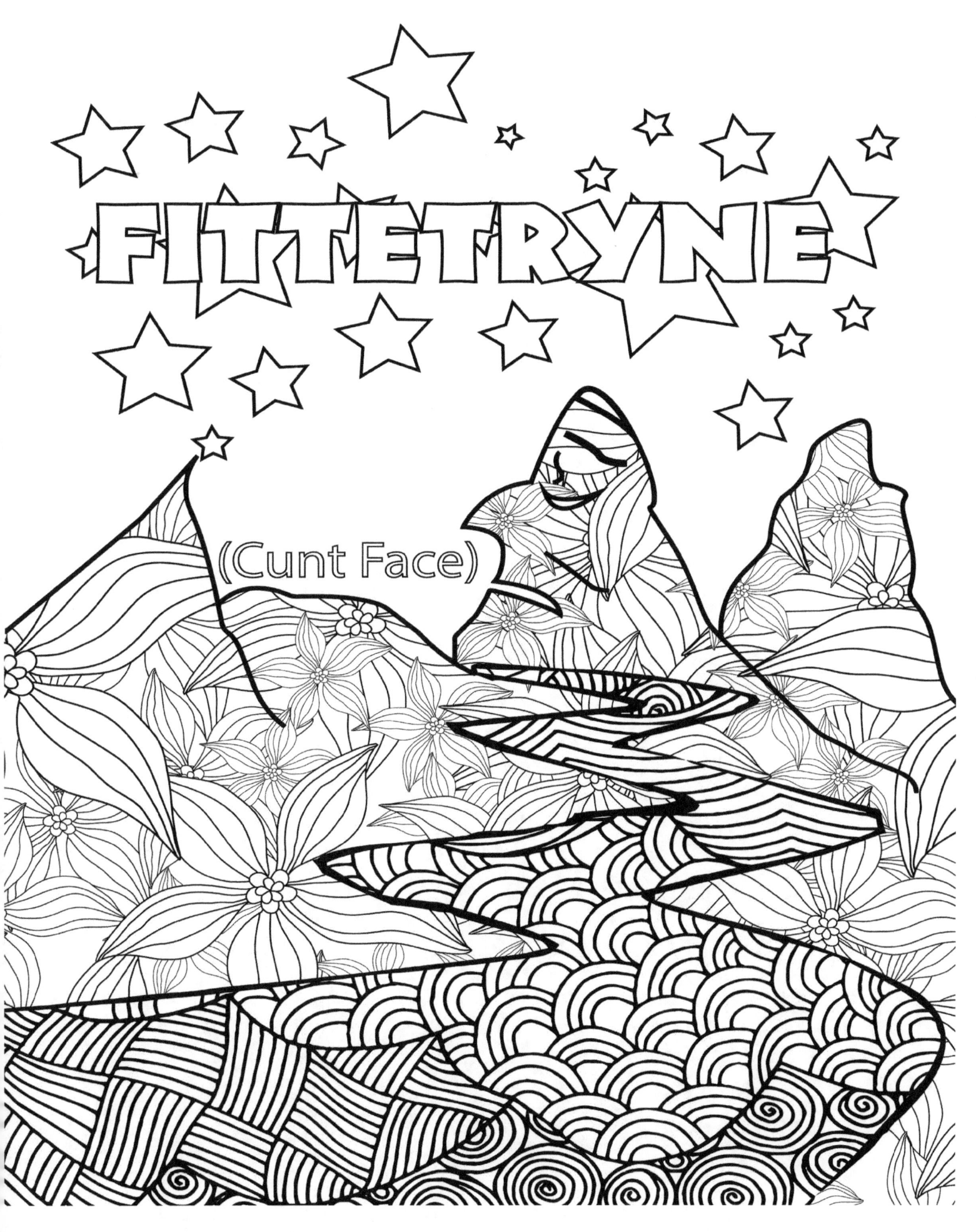

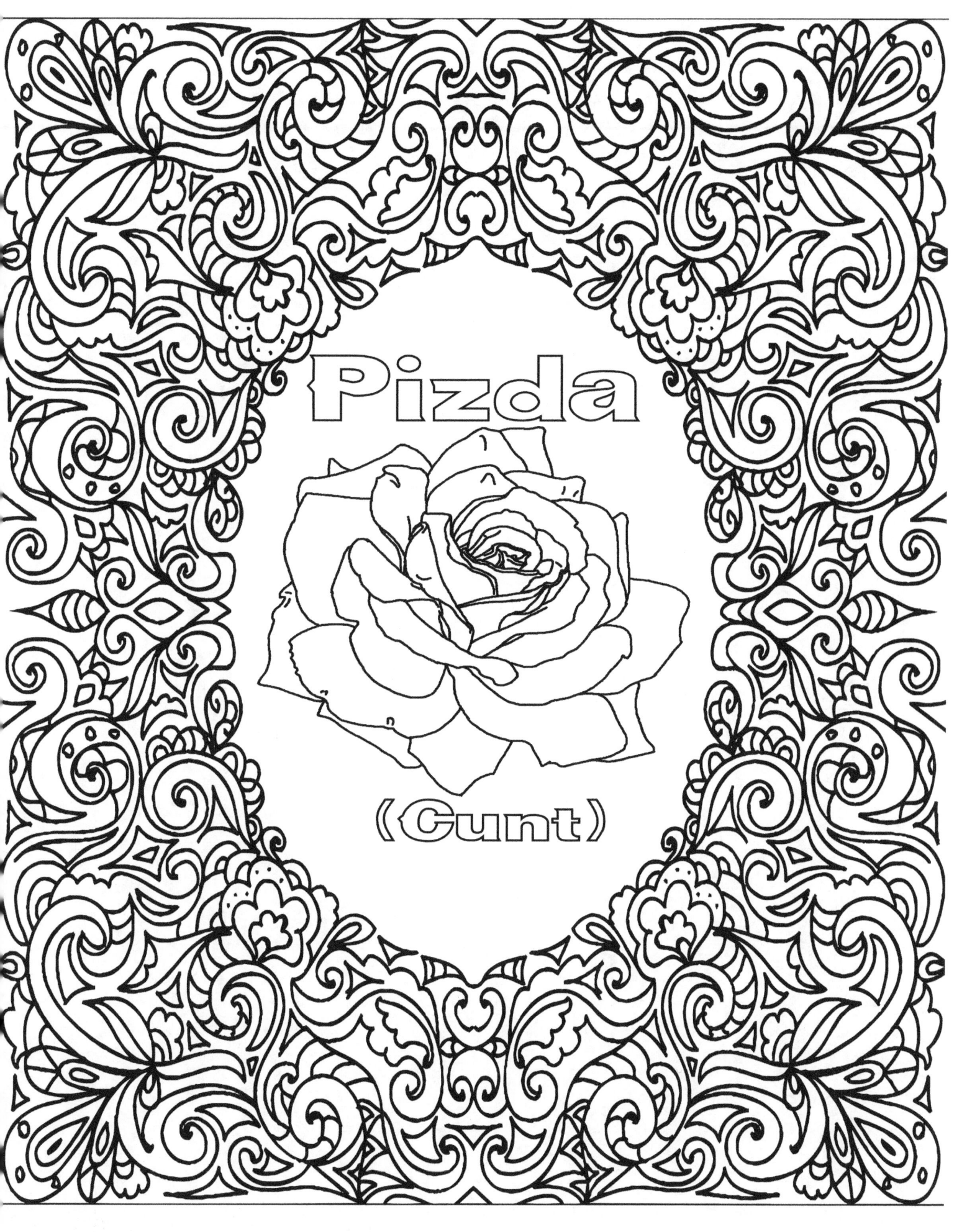

Pizda

(Cunt)

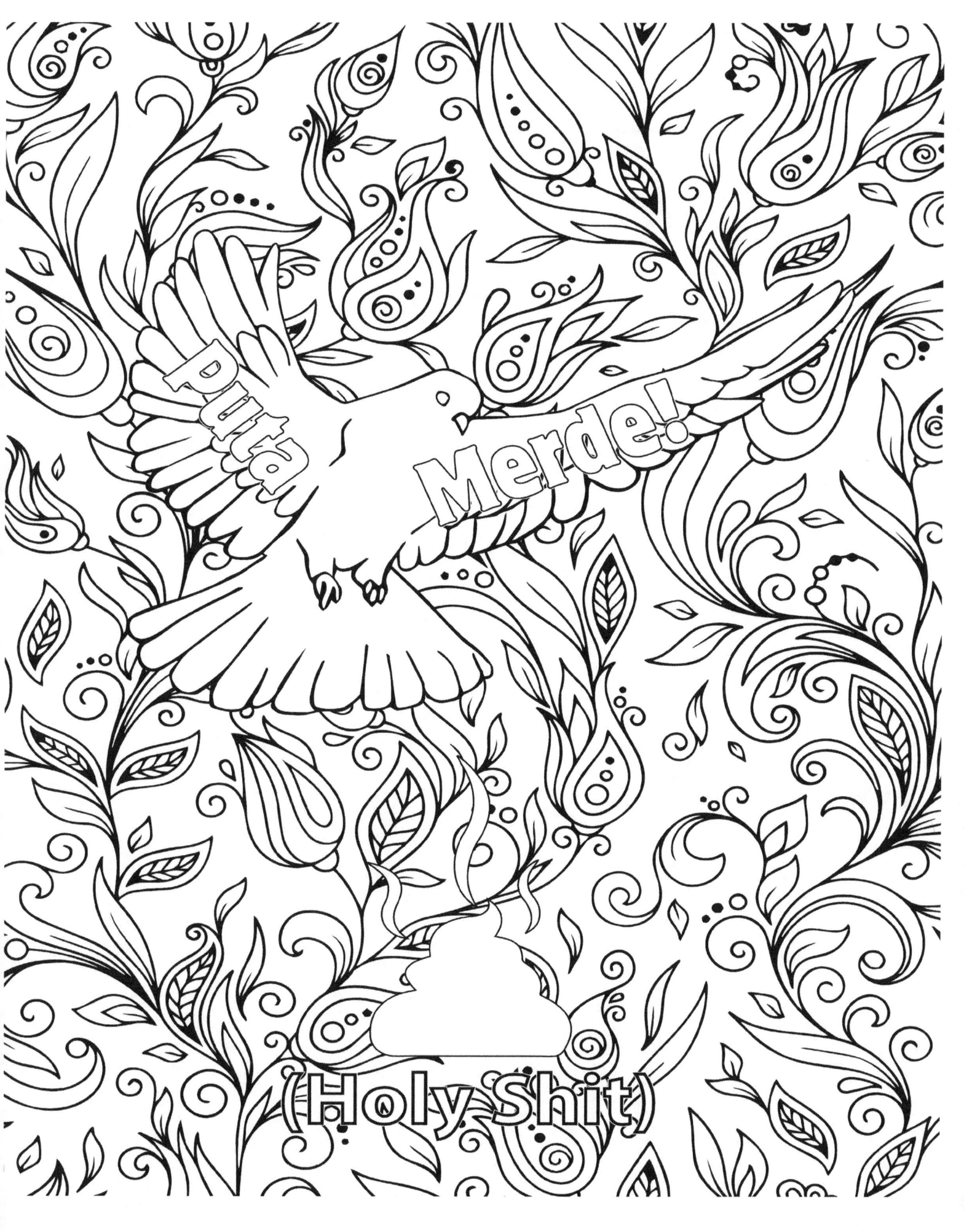

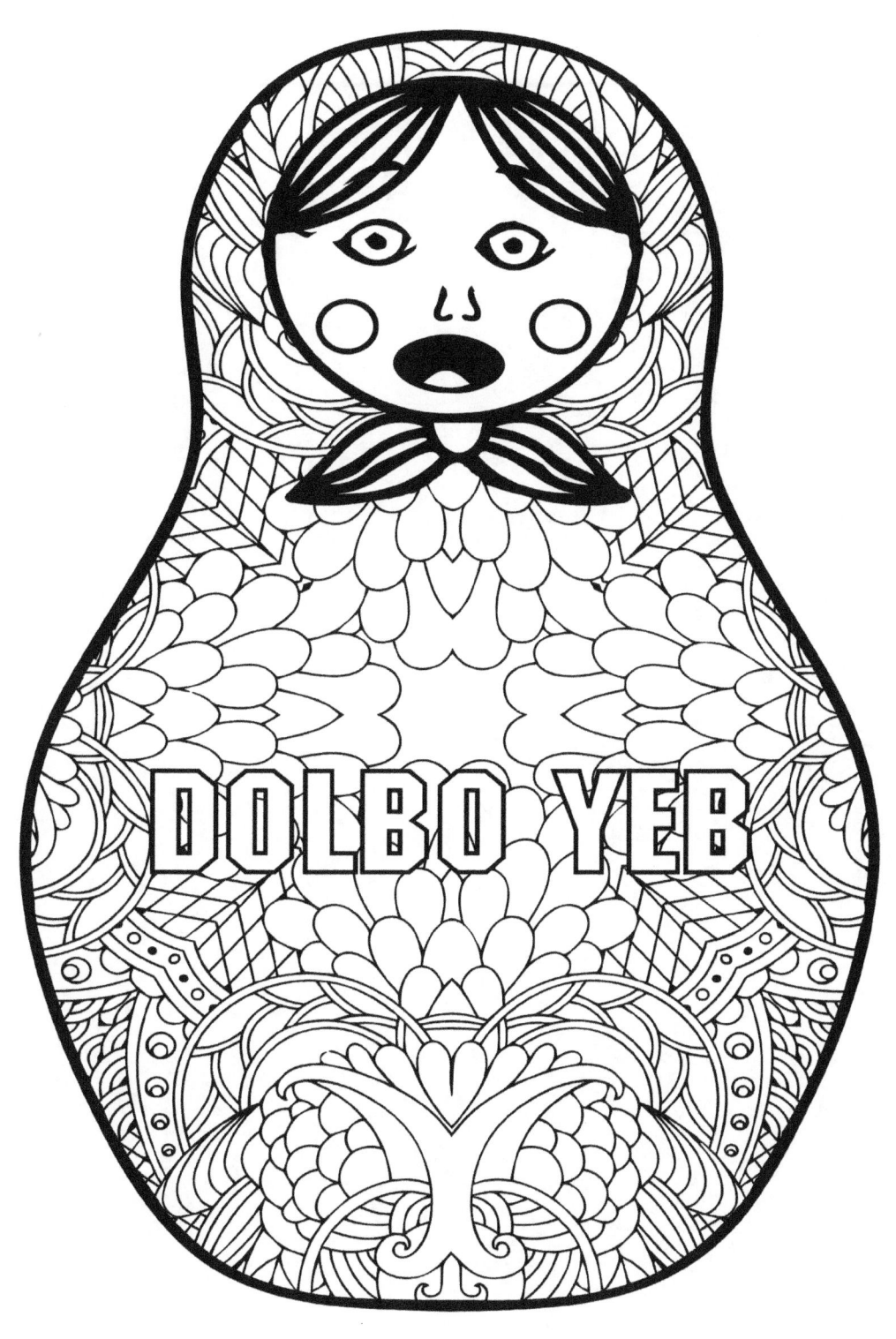

DOLBO YEB

(Dumb Fuck)

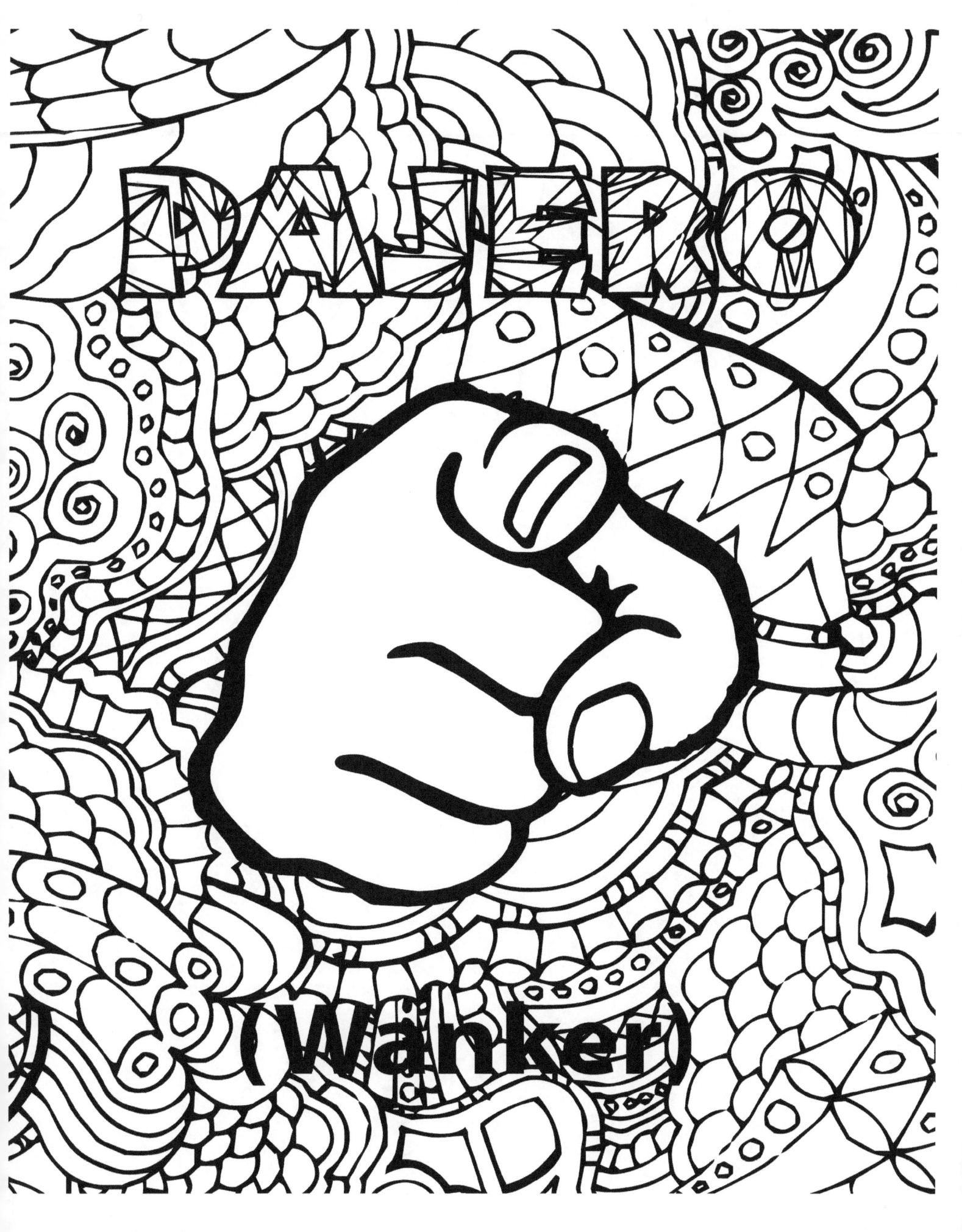

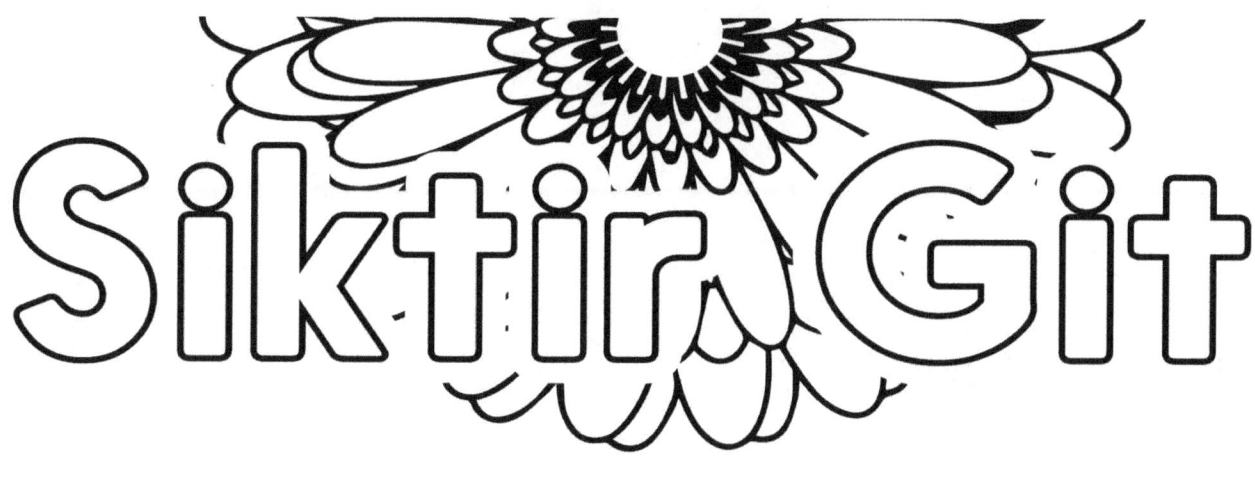

Siktir Git

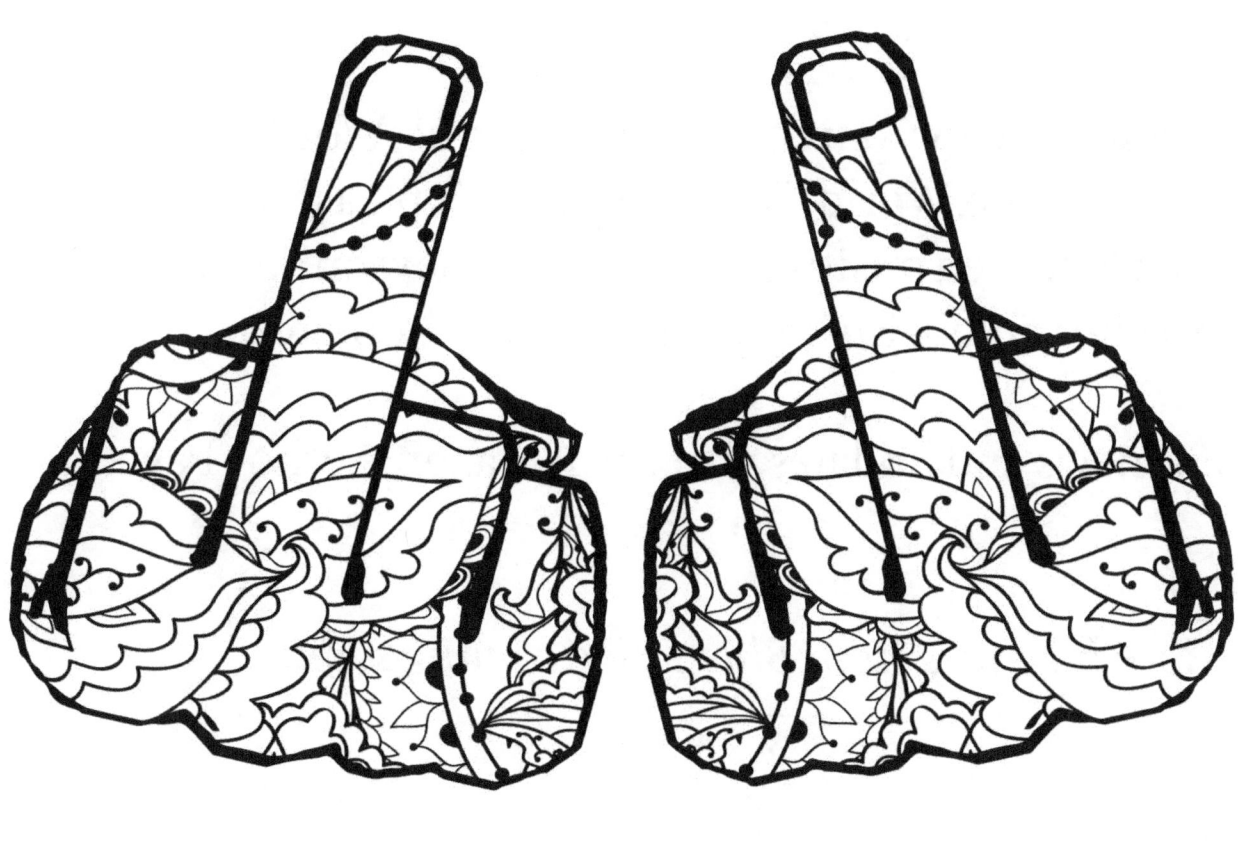

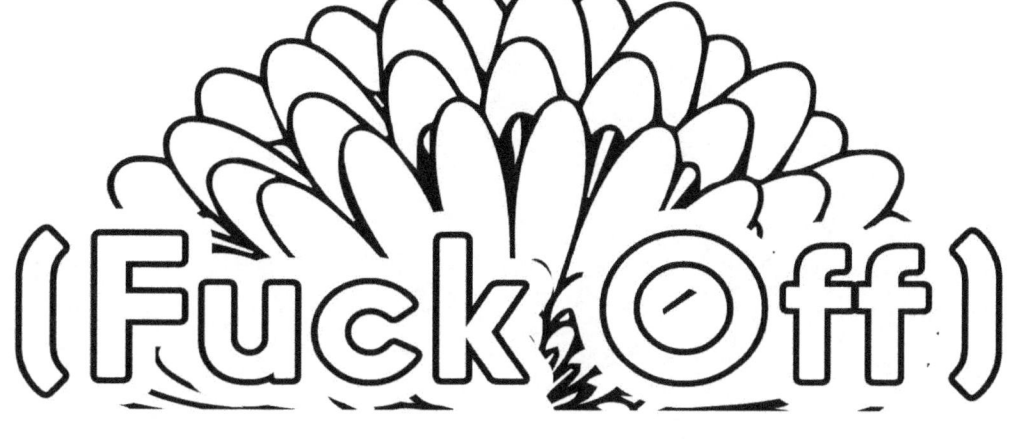

(Fuck Off)

THANK YOU!

Thank you for purchasing Colourful Words From Around The World. If you enjoyed it please take the time to leave a positive rating and review on Amazon, so other colourists may discover the book too.

For news and updates visit my Amazon Author Page.

More fun titles from Blue Paige coming soon!